THICKER.

K Winters

THICKER.

THICKER.
Take a trip into my mind.
Crack open all the intricate ways of my being.
Peel back my skin and uncover what truly lies inside.
Search head to toe for the dimensions of my soul.
Dig deep into my chest and find the madness to my loving.
Disregard my eye color and see past my body figure.
Trust me, what lies inside is much thicker.

Would've
I would have resurrected life into barren wastelands for you
I would have planted my seed in nuclear grounds for you
I would have watered concrete until flowers grew for you
But you never let me love you
Why wouldn't you?

THICKER.

Reignition
You ignited a fire in my soul
and never stuck around for the upkeep.
I can't explain the ache that grew inside
when you let that fire die
and reignited it every other night.

K WINTERS

You know, sometimes

Sometimes I wonder if you remember
all the pieces of myself I gave to you.
Do you count them the way I do?

Sometimes I wonder if you ever
planned on giving them back.
Or do you have too much pride for that?

Sometimes I wonder if you knew
what I was giving up.
But do you give a fuck about that?

THICKER.

2 am thoughts
Was she not enough of the right stuff?
Or too much of the wrong?
Was she just a temporary fix for loneliness?
Or was the timing off?
Was she second next to Mary Jane?
Or farther down the line?
Was it ever love?
Or just a burst of lust?

Either way, you left her damaged in the dust.

K WINTERS

I find love in your presence, even though it's evanescent.

I find truth in your eyes, even though they lie.

I find comfort in your arms, even though it's false.

THICKER.

Why do I still want you
when I know you're not what I want?

-A matter of love and logic

K WINTERS

Unfinished Business

'Some things are meant to be left unfinished'

I tell myself this every damn day,

in hopes that I might come to believe it.

I find reasons for everything that happens,

but I can't seem to figure out why God left

your face engraved in my mind and

the taste of your lips lingering upon mine.

THICKER.

Somehow,

you never fail

to creep into my thoughts

and remind me of how much

I wanted to be the one

you never let go.

Maybe

Maybe if I had waited a little longer,
time could have fixed the wound
that our love had become.

Maybe if I had tried a little harder,
I could have learned
to love you the way I once did.

Maybe if I had prayed a little more,
God could have answered the questions
I didn't know how to ask.

THICKER.

No one ever will

I look for parts of you in everyone,

but no one quite measures up,

and I wonder why I couldn't stay

if there were parts of you that I loved.

Identity

You were so deeply rooted into me

that I thought if I left you,

I'd lose myself.

I was afraid that leaving you

meant leaving me.

My fingerprints would no longer be mine

because, somehow, over time

ours had intertwined.

My reflection wouldn't look like me

because as I fell in love with you,

I faded from my own view.

I found that I remained the same person,

and I can only assume you did too.

THICKER.

Ashes

Our love was a fire.

It burned bright

and I was lost

in the beauty of the flames.

I felt the warmth kiss my face.

I may have been foolish

to get that close,

but I couldn't resist you.

Somehow our fire died,

and I was left with

the third-degree pain

of figuring out why.

And so, I sat,

and watched the ashes of our love

fall from the sky.

Moving on to me

I had to let go of the parts of me that were hurting
and bury the memories that caused the pain.

This gave me perspective.

I found that life went on,
and that I am the same person without you.

Moving on to me was easy,
even though you'd hoped it wouldn't be.

THICKER.

Your image was erased

from the depths of my memory,

your voice stopped echoing

against every aspect of my brain,

and your name no longer bled

from the beating organ inside my chest.

-When I chose forgiveness

Paths crossed

I see the beauty in our demise because

I know in the end we were only meant to rise.

God lead you to my presence

so that you could learn to strive

and he walked with me into your heart

so that I could learn to love right.

I see the purpose in our story

because I know we're on our paths to glory.

THICKER.

THE DIVINE

You are the most divine thing God has put in my life.

Yet, you are also the most divine thing He has taken away.

By loving you,

He taught me to love another.

By leaving you,

He taught me to love myself.

Never Love

A love that takes form in smiles,
but is never given a name.
We were just two kids that
weren't sure what it was or why,
but enjoyed making each other laugh—
within one another's reach,
but never in each other's grasp.

THICKER.

Estimated Time of Arrival

We talked about where we want to go with this

and didn't quite reach a destination,

but I crave your presence.

So, we don't need a map

to give us direction

because we chose the road

that has no expectations.

On Paper

I want to put him on paper,

so I can have a piece of him forever.

I want to write about his smile,

because it excites and calms my soul.

I want to write about his laugh

because it gives my heart a beat to dance to.

I want to write about him

simply because I feel the need to.

THICKER.

Maybe
we're just meant
for each other's egos.
Which would be fine if
we wouldn't have gone too far.
You said it was in the moment,
but I can't seem to
live outside of that time.
I thought it would be fine;
that I wouldn't get caught up
because it was you.
I thought the moment would end
and we wouldn't have to pretend
to have feelings.
But I'm not pretending.
In the moment,
I seemed to have forgotten
that I am a lover
and have a natural tendency to care.
Now that I'm invested in you,
I wish I could take back
the night I gave myself to you.
I get this feeling of disgust
when I think about
how little it meant to you.

K WINTERS

Prisoner

I am a secret locked away in a cell.

I was found guilty and you charged me life without parole.

I don't want to be a secret defined by steel cuffs.

I don't want to feel things that never go beyond brick walls.

I don't want to love you from behind bars.

So, hear my appeal or sentence me to the chair,

because I won't be a secret;

I'm done with this affair.

THICKER.

Cross my heart and hope to die
Mom always told me
to never make promises I can't keep.
So, I bite my tongue often
and, choose each word with care.
I don't speak to fill silence
because I see no reason in
creation without purpose.

Half empty

Your lack of wholeness

makes me want to have you more.

With each kiss, I could fill you

until you've forgotten

how it feels to be half full.

THICKER.

All of You

I want every aspect of you.

every shade

every smile

every mood

every shape

every flaw

every laugh

every tear

every fight

every day

I want all of you.

Presque Vu

The words are on the tip of my tongue

at every waking moment.

Pounding inside my chest,

they long to be set free.

I look at you and I swear,

my heart beats to the rhythm

of those three syllables.

I love you.

And I wonder if you feel it too.

THICKER.

Blessings

Your little flower will soon bloom.

Her petals will bless the earth with beauty.

Her stem will strengthen her for the seasons to come.

Her roots will keep her close to those that love.

Your little flower, I hope blossoms to be just like you.

Bad Intentions

I want to

overdose you with loyalty,

drown you in consistency,

burn you with honesty,

ravish you in trust,

and

strangle you with love.

THICKER.

Priorities

I want you,
but I want Him first.
I need you,
but I need Him too.
I love you,
but I love Him more.

K WINTERS

Little Eyes

Mama you're so strong;
skin rough and heart soft.
You raised three kids on your own.

Mama you're so stubborn;
hard head and narrow vision.
You never think past your own opinion.

Mama you're so loving;
bank broke and always giving.
You'll provide as long as you're living.

Mama you're so beautiful;
bright smile and high cheekbones.
You brighten up rooms.

Mama you're so crazy;
emotions high and sanity low.
You ride your own rollercoaster.

Mama I'm just like you.
I've always been watching.
What did you expect me to do?

THICKER.

To the man I will love forever
You taught me to be strong,
showed me right from wrong,
& loved me as if I was your entire world.

K WINTERS

Raise a Glass

for the women

with consistency embedded in their bones.

who love without reason to.

with loyalty pumping through their veins.

who sing when they are blue.

with hope reflecting in their eyes.

who smile their way through.

with light living within their hearts.

who turn their vulnerability into art.

THICKER.

Ma Soeur

My intention isn't to come down hard on you.

I see the woman you could be,

in hopes you're nothing like me

& I know that's exactly what you want to be.

To everyone I've ever hurt,

Forgive me for the words I shouldn't have said,

the ones I should've but never did,

and the ones that came too late.

THICKER.

Premature

My flower knowingly awakened before spring

when she wasn't yet ready to bloom,

and foolishly expected the kiss of the sun.

Her petals sprouted outward in desire,

searching for a warmth she had never known.

Its warmth had caressed her,

but not in the way that made her grow.

She watched the beauty of her petals fade

and wondered why the sun didn't make her whole.

Cleanse

Scalding hot

the water burns

turning my hair skin

into shades of hell itself

all in an attempt to rid me

of the disappointment in myself

THICKER.

FIFTY YEARS

Pour into me all your fears.

Pour into me the pain never spoken to ears.

Pour into me the words that brought you to tears.

Pour into me all the suffering of your fifty years.

Green eyes

As I stare into your green eyes

with red blotches all over my face,

I feel the warm streams of tears

trickle down my swollen cheeks.

My heart has never felt

such a stinging sorrow

as when I watched yours break.

I have never seen you so exposed;

your heart so open—bleeding.

I saw how much love has broken you.

A voice inside me screamed.

I wanted to bury your suffering within me,

so I'd never have to see

the hurt reside in your eyes;

the same green eyes as mine.

THICKER.

My tears turned my face into canvas.

Puffy eyes gave me texture.

Blotchy skin gave me pattern.

Frowned lips gave me shape.

-Your daughter's face

Love for a Summer

we first met

an instant connect

smile bright as the sun

soul as warm as she is too

laughs we shared & tears as well

fleeting in time, but ours for eternity

you'll forever be my summertime lover.

THICKER.

Logic v Love

We make sense logically.

In my head, it's all right.

The numbers add up

T's are crossed.

I's are dotted.

Not in my heart.

My pulse is a bore.

Butterflies don't soar.

Baby, loving you's a chore.

Mirage

I thought I wanted this to end...

But how do I know if it's real or pretend,

when my mind's playing tricks on my heart again?

THICKER.

SEARCH

We search and search for the good in people.

We bend over backwards to find it.

We stretch until our insides tear.

We refuse to believe it's not there.

REVIVAL

She loved him back to life.

She gave his soul a pulse once again.

She won't help him find it this time around.

She can't love him back to life while she drowns.

THICKER.

Hollow

Shell of a love I once was

empty of a heart I once loved

left hollow with half a soul, so corrupt.

Changes

I am not the lover you remember me to be.

I'm not as trusting.

I doubt the too good to be.

I no longer love without restrictions.

Boundaries seem to be my thing.

I catch myself before drifting too far.

Being lost in love isn't fun anymore.

THICKER.

Gone Girl

I let too many in,

until I'm crowded.

I let them stay too long,

until I lose my sanity.

I let them get too close,

until I miss my own space.

I let them have too many parts of me,

until I've gone away.

K WINTERS

Obituary

I buried the version of me that accepts second-hand 'love'.
She's six feet underground half as cold as your heart.
Don't go looking for the girl you had.
She's finally, truly dead.

THICKER.

I pray you

never doubt the beauty in your freckles

and find your missing pieces in the loveliest of places.

never give up the parts of yourself that you adore

and look for love in the soul, not in the eyes.

never let that big heart shrink

and always laugh uncontrollably.

K WINTERS

20/20

Sitting outside with vision so blurry,

I can only tell what's around me from memory.

At first, I was afraid my lack of sight

made me prey to everything that goes bump in the night.

The wind whirled up a whistling of the trees,

then blew away all my unease.

Lights glowed like urban flowers of the night,

and shadows were works of art on black pavement canvas.

Gazing down a fuzzy street,

I found the beauty in not being able to see.

THICKER.

TAILLIGHTS

…And he kisses my hand goodbye,

then drives off for the last time,

while playing the song of him and I.

Standing in the middle of the street,

I watch his taillights as he leaves

and wipe the tears from my cheeks.

-This is meant to be

K WINTERS

Hibiscus Love

She was scalding hot

and full of delicate flavor;

arousing senses

and changing behavior.

She was a beverage like no other.

Wanting to be wanted,

she let many take a sip.

Until one day,

she had poured her hibiscus love into so many,

there was but one last drop.

And she gave it away

because that's the kind of love she was.

THICKER.

Deeper.

No one can love deeper than they're willing to sink.

I am

I am sweet where I was bitter.

I am strong where I was withered.

I am alive where I was numb.

I am full where I was gone.

I am wild where I was tamed.

I am love where I was hate.

THICKER.

Other Side

I wonder if there is a place

where grass is really greener

and love never dies.

I wonder if I'd recognize it

by the bright blue skies

and lack of late night lies.

I wonder if I ever found it

that I'd be looking into your eyes.

K WINTERS

Perpetual Love

My dad once told me about
the first time he had laid eyes on my mom.
A divorce and twenty-five years later,
he still swears she's the most
beautiful woman he's ever seen.
If our love is doomed,
I hope it goes something like theirs—
Where the love never dies,
but it wasn't strong enough
to keep their bodies tied.
So, they had to let go
and realize that
loving isn't always from up close,
and that distance
doesn't always mean letting go.

THICKER.

Letters to the Sky

From earlobes to cheekbones,
I am a part of you
and there's nothing else I'd rather be.
The blood flowing through these veins
is as much yours as it is mine,
and there's no other blood I'd want to bleed.
These eyes that you gave me
don't share your same vision
and it's a shame you'll never
see yourself the way I do.
The color of this fair skin is
nowhere near the pigment of yours.
You'd be proud of that, but there's
nothing more I'd wish to change
than the tone of this pale face.
The hands you passed down to me
are aching from hard work,
and I'd count every crack
for a chance to have you back.
These lips only wish to speak truth
and can't help but stutter when I talk to you
because I never got to tell you
how proud I am to be a part of you.

K WINTERS

You live on in these veins,

through these eyes,

with these hands,

and by these lips.

The pieces of you that are inside

of me are the fragments that

I hold onto so desperately.

THICKER.

Destinations

Women with scars

tend to roam far.

Not from any place,

but from their own hearts.

K WINTERS

Roots.

My darling girl,

our roots are the same;

searching for underground rain,

but always end up finding pain.

THICKER.

estro|gen|erations

A masterpiece derived

from generations upon generations

of women before her;

carrying them over her shoulders.

Passion

You are embedded within my bones.

Deep in the marrow of my soul.

Nourishing my being.

Making her whole.

THICKER.

Déjà vu

He touches me

and I compare it to you;

how your fingers caressed me

oh, so smooth.

He kisses me

and I swear I taste your lips;

how your tongue was so sweet

a sugar only for me.

He holds me

and I wish it was your body;

how it wrapped around me

almost becoming a part of me.

Converse

He speaks of love leaving him raw. He speaks of the parts of his heart he thinks he has lost. He speaks of broken promises too sharp to touch. He speaks of the reasons he no longer trusts. He speaks of the ways in which he's fucked up. He speaks of his heart being cold. He speaks of his soul growing old. He speaks of butterflies that no longer exist. He speaks of being too far gone to fix.

THICKER.

She speaks of kissing his scars, so he forgets where they are. She speaks of finding them and never letting them get lost again. She speaks of picking up the pieces, so he'll never be cut by his past. She speaks of her love and how it is sacred. She speaks of the ways she can love him back to life. She speaks of thawing his heart because hers is the sun. She speaks of awakening his soul, so it'll never grow old. She speaks of resurrections through kisses and long talks. She speaks of being let in, so she can show him how beautiful the world is again.

K WINTERS

Vision

When the rain pours down,

I find you beside me.

As drops run down your skin,

I swear they create words.

Following the trails they leave,

'I love you' is soaking into your face.

After wiping the water from my eyes,

I find that my vision was fine.

Those words have been written

on your skin the whole time.

THICKER.

Religion

Boy, you are godly.

Your lips are a piece of heaven on earth;

blessing me with every kiss you steal from me.

How can you sin and do it angelically?

K WINTERS

Substance

I need a love of substance

that burns for an eternity;

fuel for the fire

that's burning within me.

THICKER.

Beginnings

I want to lose sight
of where my body ends
and yours begins.

05/04

You have given me life.

No, I don't mean birth

because anyone can do that.

You have fallen to your knees for me,

broken your back to support me,

risen from hell to save me,

and given your life to raise me.

You have been breathing life into these lungs

without thinking of your own

and putting food in this mouth

before reaching for your own.

THICKER.

The American Dream

Cracking under the pressure
Is this what we're meant for?
We've become slaves
to what teachers have been
preaching since the first grade.
Paper after paper after paper
to be thrown in a cage
filled with underlying rage and
locked by their expectations
to grow up 'living' on minimum wage.
Paycheck to paycheck to paycheck
with nothing to show for our broken homes
and no one that cares about our withering bones
because this is how they want us to live,
or more importantly die.
They don't want to witness life
that began in the gutters
and fought for the day
that their children no longer
get written out of school plays
because 'God doesn't love their race'.
Fought for the day that their children
smile in the face of the giant

and no longer remain silent
about the horrors of how
their people have been raised
to believe that
culture is something to be ashamed
and that color is to blame
for poverty, bloodshed, and pain.
But they can't expect us to be silent
when they are the ones who have slain
all people with melanin in their veins,
hidden it in the hearts of those who witnessed it,
and waited until the memories of their crimes have died
so they can write history in their twisted light,
forever denying the murder of thousands of lives
within the pages of books
we break our backs and fall to our knees
to pay for our children to memorize.
The American dream.

THICKER.

SEP|A|RATE

You and I are so different.

A knock at the door is welcome for me,

but for you that sound is uncertainty.

You grew up thinking that cops are the enemy,

but, for me, they represented security.

I've made a habit out of trusting,

but you've lived your life half-way out the door.

Is this meant to be?

We're separate worlds, you and me.

But, I guess, there's nothing else I'd rather be.

Self-Inflicted

I cannot write the words to explain
how it hurts to watch you inflict pain
on your own heart and into your own veins.
Letting men beat you until your insides are raw;
fully aware of the damage they'll cause,
you never seem to push pause.
If we accept the love we think we deserve,
your definition must be twisted and curved
because you do not have to sub serve
for someone to look at you and see their whole world.
Obedience and love are not on the same spectrum.
What has made you romanticize
loving men that traumatize
and only love you through insincere apologies?

THICKER.

This hollow feeling inside my chest
is demanding to be noticed;
demanding to be set free
but I can't find the words
to let this feeling escape me.
It grows and grows in size and mass,
weighing heavier on my ribs,
until I can no longer stand.

He
is rain
against
a tin roof
and the ray
of light that
shines through

He
is the
rosy of
my cheeks
and the whisper
of my breath when
I am soundly asleep

He
is the
taste of
honey and
the sound of
a summer breeze
whistling through trees

THICKER.

Holy Practices

So pure,

his love is baptism.

I drown in the depths

of his holy water, and

pray for air to find my chest.

On the brink of death,

he breathes life into my hopeless lungs

and once again, I become the woman in love.

-He is both my demise and my resurrection

K WINTERS

Ablaze
The heat of our bodies
could burn whole cities.

THICKER.

Fathers

It's quite tragic, isn't it?

Fathers leave behind the best part of themselves

and come to find that she has grown up,

but has no idea all the struggles it took.

He missed the little things that molded her into a whole

and then claims to be proud,

but doesn't know what for.

Dads are supposed to be lifetime loves

and teach their daughter what that means,

but he never stuck around to show her what that was.

So, instead, she came to believe that love was conditional

and that it's okay for men to leave

if she didn't have what they need.

It's quite tragic, isn't it?

K WINTERS

FLESH AND BONES

I live in this skin every day.

I carry this flesh with these bones.

I bear this weight with these toes.

I hold this head high on my shoulders.

This skin

these bones

this chest

these breasts

this tummy

these hips

this chin

& these lips

are mine to decide

what I can and cannot

should and should not

will or will not

do with them.

A man cannot choose

what I shall do with my body

until he's carried my flesh and bones,

bore my weight with his toes,

and held my head on his shoulders.

THICKER.

Prosthetic Love

I am sowing the right seeds in the worst of places;

The sun doesn't shine and water doesn't flow.

These seeds are my heart

and when I planted them in your soil,

I thought you'd help them grow

but you swallowed them whole

and kept them in darkness for the world to never know.

So, I'm left with my seeds in the ground

and your never-ending drought,

still with the hope that you'll foster

the love I've planted in you.

Our souls could've intertwined

like wild vines weaving through time—

which is what I thought we were,

but no matter how ready they were to grow,

 oh, so wild and beautiful for you,

you couldn't nurture the seeds I left in your earth.

I believed I was growing with you.

All the while, you were

replacing the sun with lightbulbs

and water with bleach—

we weren't alive at all;

just a perfectly structured,

K WINTERS

plastic and synthetic version

of what love is supposed to be.

You tricked me

and as much as I hate to admit it,

it was the best love story I had ever seen.

THICKER.

TRUST|ED

I trust you

I trust the good in you

I trust beyond reasonable doubt

I trust until I'm given reason not to

I trust because I want to give you a chance

I trust that you will recognize what you have

I trusted that you would recognize what you had

I trusted because I wanted to give you a chance

I trusted until you gave me reason not to

I trusted you beyond reasonable doubt

I trusted the good in you

I trusted you

You always said I trusted too easily and loved too much, but I never expected that you would be the one to prove it.

K WINTERS

Legs

Limbs

Intertwined

Bound

Tied

To you

To me

To each other

Until our bones wither

And our minds retire

THICKER.

Paced

Losing me is not sudden.

It is not fiery passion

or rivers of bitter tears.

It is slow and paced

because a heart like mine

cannot choose to end

something so divine

through one-sided arguments

caused by my hard-headed mind.

You lose me over time.

Day to day of emotional neglect.

Bit by fucking bit of broken promises.

Until there is nothing left,

but a single tear

that accepts defeat.

Because you see,

it was never my intention

to leave.

K WINTERS

Loving a Black Man in America
Anger and frustration
Rage and abolition
Eyes of confusion
Looks of wonder
Stares of judgement
Family disownment
Discomfort in predominantly white places
Defying racism daily
Realizing people you love are racist
Debating wedding invitations
Reconsidering your relationships
Fearing your father won't love his grandkids
Complication on family occasion
Fighting societal expectations

Absolutely worth it.

THICKER.

Tr|US|t

I shattered the glass.

Now, frantically trying to put the shards back,

my hands are decorated with wounds;

open and bleeding—

in the process of healing.

Much like our love;

open and bleeding—

in the process of healing.

Healing—
You
Me
Us
Trust

K WINTERS

WAR

This war within myself

is an unending hell.

My heart goes to battle,

but can never return victoriously

for it is waging war on itself.

THICKER.

War on Women

We carry our mothers

and her mother

and her mother

and her mother.

Generations and generations

of women we hold on our shoulders.

The beauty.

The strength.

The oppression.

Each woman fights the same battle—

that her mind, her strength, her influence,

all matter.

The twenty-first century woman is no more free

than she was in 1919

because a misogynist does not have to declare war

against estrogen to believe a woman is less than.

Less than.

Less than.

Less than.

Ideas, thoughts, and beliefs

bar us in cuffs and chains

just as much, if not more,

than a man who openly declares his hate for women

K WINTERS

because harboring weapons in silence
does far more damage
than openly declaring war
on mothers, sisters, daughters, and lovers.

YOUR MOTHERS
YOUR SISTERS
YOUR DAUGHTERS
YOUR LOVERS.

THICKER.

Heads Up
You were going to do what you wanted.
You always did anyway.
The least you could've done though,
was let me know it wasn't me anymore.

K WINTERS

RAW
Unfilled eyebrows
Undone hair
Natural lashes
Comfy underwear
Bare face
Wide eyes
Cellulite
Thick thighs
Stretch marks
And
Tan lines.

THICKER.

Love is my religion.

Feels.
Lately, I don't feel.
I haven't felt
for anything
but you
since the day
I reached out my hand
and gave myself to you.

THICKER.

Ghost Town|EMPTY
My life is empty without you
like a ghost town
that no one bothers to pass through.
Once full of movement and life,
now dead and silent and dry.
Color ceases to exist and
the wind doesn't blow, but
the sun shines hotter
than you've ever known.
It steals the water from the ground
and leaves me empty in this town
whenever you're not around.

K WINTERS

Value
What breaks her down
into believing her value
comes from a man?
Living her life
for the affirmations of others.
Others—
who do not know
the contents of her soul.

THICKER.

It can take you on vibrant,
soul elevating, life altering trips
and leave you flat on your face with
a sobriety so intense you never
want to feel the high again.

L o v e

Vulnerability
I opened up for you,
like a flower in full bloom.
I made myself vulnerable to you
by showing you my petals,
but more so,
by showing you my thorns.

THICKER.

Forget
I made you cry
when I walked away;
rivers of tears
flowing down your face,
leaving traces of our love in their place.

K WINTERS

Sunken
I never wanted this to end.
I didn't board a ship I believed was sinking.
I thought that every Titanic has its iceberg,
but it was us.
There was no iceberg at all,
just miscommunication
between two captains of the same ship.
You see, we thought we were
heading toward different destinations
so, ultimately, what sunk this love
is lack of communication.

THICKER.

HOME
You turned 'home'
from a place into a person.
It is no longer a destination
built upon manmade foundation.
Look at you—
a walking, breathing, talking place
to live my every day in.
Rather than hanging portraits on walls,
you wear our memories on your skin.
You. Are. Home.
Because you are where I go
when I need
protection
love
appraisal
and
affection.

Hard Headed | Soft Hearted
She is a paradoxical combination
of sympathy and contemplation.
With a hard head,
she is steadfast in decision,
but with a soft heart,
she is open to persuasion.
Logical beyond belief.
Understanding beyond relief.
She is the mind that says 'no'
and the heart that screams 'yes'.
She is the constant war waging
between logic and love,
but love always wins.

THICKER.

Stop
loving what drains you.
loving what breaks you.
loving what hurts you.
loving what hates you.

K WINTERS

Start
loving what fills you.
loving what builds you.
loving what heals you.
loving what loves you.

THICKER.

My Bones
You weathered my bones;
smoothed their edges,
and changed their form,
until I was no more.

K WINTERS

BE ABOUT LOVE.
BE EMPATHETIC.
BE VULNERABLE.
BE FRAGILE.
BE HUMAN.

THICKER.

My silence
screams louder
than any noun
you could ever
call me outside my name.

Dead love
A relationship doesn't die abruptly.
It's slow
and creeping
until one day,
you look at the person you 'love'
and no longer know what you see.

THICKER.

Waves
It's ok to love yourself in waves.
As long as you come back to shore.

K WINTERS

'Okay'
Driving to your house,
to drop off your belongings
and pick up my things,
with tear-filled eyes
I told myself that I was okay.

You held me for the last time.
Looking up, I saw the pain in your eyes.
I felt part of my heart die.

With yours on your sleeve,
you asked me to leave.

So, I got in my car and
tried to find the strength to turn the key
while I held back the urge to scream.

I couldn't believe
the love of my life was lost to me.

Driving back to my house,
after dropping off your belongings
and picking up my things,
with tear-stained cheeks
I told myself that you were okay.

I knew I was lying both times.

THICKER.

Out|Growth
I'm sorry I outgrew you.
I was just beginning to flourish
and you were depriving me.
Don't you see that you were depriving me?
Everything in me told me to go,
but you stood there with your roots in my soil
and blocked the sun so I couldn't grow.

But maybe,
You weren't trying to deprive me at all.
Maybe, just maybe,
you were only trying to be part of my growth.

K WINTERS

Nothings into somethings
She had nothing left to give you,
and somehow,
you found a way to take that too.

THICKER.

And now she's
scratching,
screaming,
fighting,
pleading
to crawl out of love.

K WINTERS

Betrayal
Simple.
Black and white.
You cross the line
or you don't.
Unfortunately for us, I did.
I stabbed you in the back
with the blade of trust
then took it out
and expected you not to bleed out.
Now I'm asking why you're down and out,
but the answer is simple.
I betrayed you.

THICKER.

As a little girl
trying to find
her place in this world,
my eyes were on you.
They always have been.
How could you not see
that my little world
began and ended at your feet?

K WINTERS

When the heart speaks,
time ceases to matter.

THICKER.

GENDER ROLES

Being a woman is emotion.
Being a woman is sexualization.
Being a woman is strength.
Being a woman is soft.
Being a woman is masculinity.
Being a woman is promiscuity.
Being a woman is intellect.
Being a woman is conformity.
Being a woman is freedom.
Being a woman is passion.
Being a woman is struggle.
Being a woman is fear.
Being a woman is courage.

K WINTERS

Being a woman is satisfaction.
Being a woman is sacredness.
Being a woman is weakness.
Being a woman is hard.
Being a woman is femininity.
Being a woman is prudence.
Being a woman is beauty.
Being a woman is revolutionary.
Being a woman is oppression.
Being a woman is apathy.
Being a woman is adversity.
Being a woman is dauntlessness.
Being a woman is cowardice.

Being a woman is whatever the fuck she wants it to be.

THICKER.

Female Experience
Emotions dismissed as 'pms'
Promiscuity determined by dress
Reproductive rights debated amongst men
Uncomfortable looks at the gym
Pressure to be thick or thin
Expectations to have perfect skin
Holding your breath while passing men on the sidewalk
Avoiding eye contact and small talk
Walking to the car with your keys in hand
Looking over your shoulders at night
'wearing clothes too tight' means justified victimization
Being a victim of rape leads to social ostracization
But only if you choose not to suffer in silence
Because a woman's voice is only valued if it's congruent to a man's.

K WINTERS

TOUCH
I touch my own flesh and hate what I feel
because my heart is only trying to heal,
but the blood my people gave me
keeps trying to 'save me'
from loving a man made of melanin
and making him my husband
because I'll ruin their bloodline
with my little Haitian children.
To disown your only daughter
because she loves a man of color,
is ignorance at its finest.
I refuse to let my children grow up
and believe that grandpa doesn't love them
because of the tone of their skin
or the texture of their hair
so, disown me if you can't love them
as much as you would without pigmentation.

THICKER.

Words
the words you struggle
to let escape your lips
and leave a bitter taste
on the tip of your tongue
the words you speak
that make your lungs sore
and weigh on your ribs
'til you can't breathe anymore
the words you can't fathom
ever bringing into existence
and cause you to suffer
alone with your thoughts in silence
are the words the world
desperately needs to hear
because they are
raw.
uncensored.
unapologetic.
human.

K WINTERS

Look at me.
Do you see?
See me as I am,
not as you want me to be.
Not as some perfect version
of myself that you perceive me to be.

THICKER.

THICKER.
Take a trip into my mind.
Crack open all the intricate ways of my being.
Peel back my skin and uncover what truly lies inside.
Search head to toe for the dimensions of my soul.
Dig deep into my chest and find the madness to my loving.
Disregard my eye color and see past my body figure.
Trust me, what lies inside is much thicker.

Made in the USA
San Bernardino, CA
03 June 2018